World of
HORSES

For Paul White
a friend in need
(and fond of horses too)

World of
HORSES

Caroline Silver

OMEGA BOOKS

Contents

Series edited by Howard Loxton
Picture research by Ann Davies

This edition published 1983 by Omega Books Ltd,
1 West Street, Ware, Hertfordshire, under licence
from the proprietor.

Copyright © 1976 Elsevier Publishing Projects SA, Lausanne.

ISBN 0 907853 34 X

Printed and bound in Hong Kong by South China Printing Co.

Introduction

Lord Poseidon, from you this pride is ours:
The strong horses, the young horses; and also the rule of the deep.

According to Greek mythology, the first horse came from the sea. His name was
Arion and he was the son of Poseidon, the god of the sea and brother of Zeus.
In the Old Testament it says: "Hast Thou given the horse strength? Hast Thou
clothed his neck with thunder? He paweth in the valley and rejoiceth in his strength."
Such tributes have been paid to horses throughout the ages of man. But why
should man care so much about an animal that James Thurber humorously
described as having "one leg at each corner"?

The answer, if there is an answer, has to do with the reverence that thousands
of years ago showed itself in the myth of the centaur, the manhorse as one being.
It is the delight of anyone who has ridden a good horse on testing country,
watched a thoroughbred move freely over open pasture, or touched the neck
of a horse and been rewarded with the richness of its texture and its scent,
the horse's patience, trust, and strength.

This book is meant as a communication between those of us who feel that way.

To Topaz, a Filly

To the human observer, the pattern of the horse's life begins at birth more than for any other domestic animal. There is no building of a nest, no anxiety, no altered behavior pattern to inform us of what is up with a pregnant mare. Some mares get fat, some don't; and many an informed horseman has gone hunting on his mare, not knowing what she was up to 11 months before—when she met a stallion on the quiet—only to find her in the box next morning with a foal at foot. The guilt he feels at having ridden her hard in that condition is unneeded: she does as many generations of her forebears have done in the wild—moves on from day to day, foals, gets up and moves again.

The process of birth is the same from breed to breed, affected only by the degree of human anxiety, emotional or financial, which fractionally alters the circumstances in which the foal is born. The following true story of a birth to Topaz, though involving the close attendance merited by a racehorse foal worth many thousands of pounds, applies fundamentally just as well to a carthorse or to a Shetland pony.

In thoroughbred racing circles the ruling is that the mare (described as "visiting") goes to the stallion (described as "resident"). The famous stud where Topaz was to foal had known many great stallions, the residents at the time of her arrival, for example, both being winners of the English Derby. Visiting mares usually foal at the stud and are then served at their first heat after foaling, this is the case on most thoroughbred stud farms. Thus Topaz, a 19-year-old chestnut mare, in foal to yet another Derby winner, arrived a few weeks before foaling so that her body could acquire immunity against local infections which might be dangerous to her foal.

Topaz belonged to a famous American owner-breeder. She was a big old mare with only one eye—the right eye had been lost through an infection—and a stomach distended by ten foalings. She was once (hard to imagine in her big-bellied old age) a winner on the racecourse.

Northern hemisphere racehorses are begotten unusually early so that they can benefit as youngsters from the artificial birthdate set for all at January 1. During the second week of March Topaz's udder "bagged up" full of milk. On March 21 she "waxed"—

a thickish secretion oozed from each milk canal and hardened into wax-like blobs on her teats. Drops of milk fell from her udder. On the morning of March 24 the muscles around her tail looked hollow and slack. Slackening, caused by the hormone *relaxin* which softens the ligaments to ease the passage of the foetus, occurs 12 to 18 hours before the foal is born and is so slight that it is easily overlooked. Topaz's excellent stud groom noticed it, however, and moved her into a foaling box.

With so much money at stake dependent on a successful birth the comfortable foaling boxes were fitted with television cameras, monitored by a control set in the sitting-up room where someone was always on watch during the foaling season. On March 24 a Dutch girl sat with the mares. At 7.45 p.m. she noticed that Topaz had broken out in a light sweat on the neck, soon spreading to a heavy sweat on the neck and girth which steamed in the cool air of the box. She called in the stud groom.

Topaz seemed calm and easy in herself. "These old mares don't upset themselves much," the stud groom explained. "Topaz knows a lot about it." At 8 o'clock she got down in her straw and rolled, breathing in short snorts of discomfort because her stomach was so large. Then she got up quickly. Colostrum, the important first milk containing antibodies to immunise the foal against disease, spurted from both teats. The groom milked a little of it into his hand, found that it was mainly milk and that Topaz had already lost most of her colostrum. He wasn't worried: he had spare colostrum in the deep freeze, milked from mares who had had plenty, and Topaz's foal could have a bottle of that.

8.10: The mare went down again, rolling. The groom reckoned that she knew the foal was not quite in the correct position and she was rolling to get it right. He washed his arms up over the elbow in warm, disinfected water and reached into her vagina to check. Topaz knuckered to him softly. Her birth canal was blocked by the partly-ejected water bag, which he burst with his hand so that he could reach through and feel that the foal was in the proper position (if not, this would be the moment to straighten it). Water poured out of Topaz, and one of the foal's forelegs stuck out from under her tail, encased in thick white membrane. The groom felt the other foreleg, lying a little behind the first and touched the head, lying neatly along both legs like a diver's. Satisfied

The birth of a thoroughbred. The mare's tail is bandaged to keep loose hairs from getting in the way.
Right: The foal's forelegs are emerging in the correct position.
Far right: A moment of rest at the end of labor. The foal's hind legs are still in the birth canal but the amniotic sac is partly off and the foal has begun to breathe.

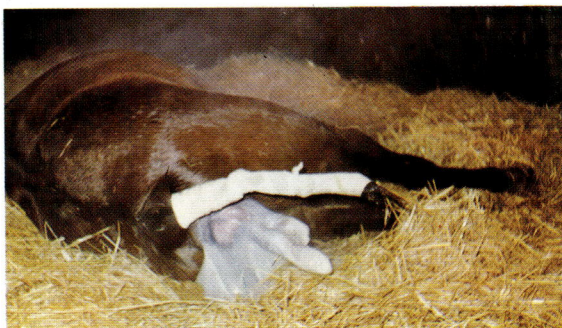

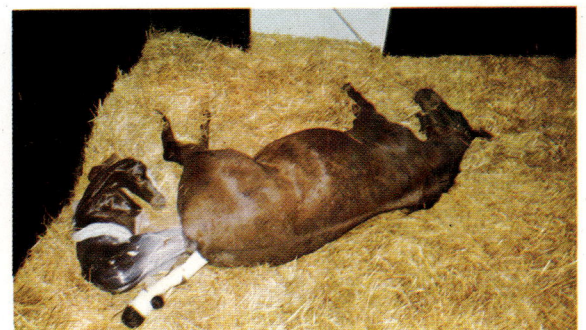

A luxury birth: the foal has been lifted to the mare's head to save her the effort of getting up to inspect it.

that the foal's shoulders would pass on a slant through the narrow pelvic area and that its nose would not get stuck against the roof of the vagina, he withdrew his arm and left the mare to get on with it by herself.

At 8.15 the other foreleg showed, just behind the first. Topaz began to work, a contraction every few seconds drawing her stomach up from underneath. She stopped and panted, blowing with pain, then stretched out on her side again. Discomfort made her twist her head so that her nose pointed towards the ceiling, and her upper lip curled back to show her teeth. One of the foal's hooves burst through the amniotic sac. The end of its foot was white and soft, and looked like flabby gristle at the tip.

8.24: The foal's head appeared, covered in membrane. When the contraction passed and Topaz had relaxed the groom pulled gently on the second foreleg, which was dragging back into the mare. The foal's nose stuck out clear of the amniotic sac, nostrils closed and tongue hanging out; it wasn't breathing yet. Lying in the straw, Topaz turned her head and hummered (her attending groom's word for the intimate voice a mare uses to her foal). "Not there yet, old girl," he told her.

Topaz bore down hard. She stuck her legs out stiff, and curled her lips back over her gums in effort. At 8.29 the foal slipped easily out, and as its ribcage slid clear of the constricting vagina it gave a little gasp and started to breathe. The groom cleared the water from its nostrils with his finger, which he said wasn't really

A strong cart mare with her newborn foal. She has given birth in the field without the watchful attention given to valuable thoroughbreds.

Horse and pony foals are always hungry.

necessary. As the foal's hind legs slipped away from the mare she got up fast and turned, eager to see her foal, snapping the umbilical cord which bled in spurts. The groom held the end of it tight between finger and thumb until the bleeding stopped.

Topaz bent over the foal, hummering to it and licking it dry. It was a bay filly, daughter of a Derby winner, a sticky little effort with a wisp of beard hanging from its lower lip and a hide soaked wet with fluid. It lay in the straw limply, buffeted from side to side by Topaz's tongue.

The mare's huge empty belly looked no smaller, but her sides were hollow below the hip. The empty placenta draggled down behind her, and the groom tied it up with binder twine to keep her from kicking at it or stepping on it.

Eight minutes from birth the foal tried to get up, rocking backwards in the straw with its forelegs splayed out in front while Topaz, hummering, licked its face. A spurt of pain got her down in her bed, rolling as the tired muscles of her stomach contracted. The stud groom and his Dutch assistant hurried to pull the foal out of the way, afraid she might roll on it accidentally.

Most foals take an hour to stand, but Topaz's strong filly was up on its feet, wobbling, in only 17 minutes. Three times it crabbed over backwards on to its bottom, but it would not give in. Topaz continued to dry it, talking to it all the time. "Funny old girl," the groom said. "You'd think an old mare like that would be used to it, but she's like a kid with a Christmas present." Topaz began to frisk a little, raising her elderly body in tiny rears of delight.

At 8.58 the afterbirth came away and the groom removed it, checking that it was complete as a partly-retained placenta can cause infection in a mare. The foal, walking now, stuck its nose out questingly towards him. "I'm not your mother," he said to it. It lurched away to Topaz, feeling along her side for the teat. It had no notion where to look. It poked its mother in the armpit, hard; she swung her head around and pushed it away, kicking out fussily. Saliva ran down the foal's lips in a fine white hungry foam; it licked its mother's udder, but didn't drink. Topaz blew air down her nose impatiently.

At 9.44 it found the teat and began to suck.

What happened thereafter is very much the same for any young foal. It is put out to pasture with its dam and with other mares and foals,

coming in at night if the weather is inclement and it is high born and roughing it outside without much harm if it isn't. It learns fast, vitally, to manage its long legs at a trot and canter, swings away up the pasture to rear and box with the other young foals; picks curiously at the grass, forelegs straddled so that it can get its short neck close enough to the turf, not really eating, more in imitation of its dam. Horses learn by imitation—so much so that a riding horse should never be fostered on a carthorse because it will pick up a clumsy galloping action.

As the summer days lengthen and the sun gets on its back it grows big and fit and starts to graze properly. In the natural way of life, today left open to very few animals, it will continue to drink from its mother either until she gets fed up with it and drives it off or until the stallion of the herd chases it away. It behaves very much as a human would under similar circumstances—hanging around miserably on the fringes of its own society, getting bitten and kicked by the bigger fellow, until eventually it joins up with a group of contemporaries or with another herd that will let it tag along. Most foals are more kindly weaned by human agency at about six months old, forcibly separated in a traumatic few hours of squeaking and screaming which is most humanely done by keeping the mare and foal out of earshot of each other; then, if lucky, turned out the next day with other foals of about the same age. The mother–child bond breaks decisively, and within only a very few weeks the mare and foal will appear not to recognize each other if they meet. The lapse of time between weaning and breaking in a young horse varies with the purpose for which it has been bred. Horses come to full physical maturity at about four years old, and a heavy weight put upon their backs before that age can cause permanent damage to the spinal column. Under the silken skin of many flat racehorses who are broken in and ridden and, in North America, even raced as yearlings, fused vertebrae are often found, though luckily this seldom seems to cause pain to the horse or affect its racing or stud career. Most horses are left to mature slowly, never feeling the weight of a human or the constriction of a saddle until they are three or four years old. During this gentle seasonal rotation of growth —through the shedding of the foal coat as the first winter approaches, the loss of the remnants of the curly foal tail which still linger in the yearling, the awkward, gangling stages in which the body grows unevenly, sometimes shooting up behind then growing up in front and looking sway-backed until the middle grows up to the same height, the growing in of a full set of temporary teeth and their slow replacements by the permanent teeth of a mature animal—the inquisitive young horse learns from experience and by examples from its associates. Wise handling, if the owner has the time to do it, means that the horse is constantly associated with man, learning elementary lessons such as to wear a halter and be led or to pick up its feet when asked and hold them steady for the hoofpick during the first few months of life, coming to the paddock gate when called and getting accustomed to the sudden buzz of traffic. (It is of immense value if a young horse can be pastured in a busy area with a wise old horse who shows no fear when a heavy truck grinds past or a train hisses and rattles at shattering speed on a nearby railway track.)

Fear of the unfamiliar is natural to a horse, whose whole survival instinct is bound up with the ability to flee from anything potentially dangerous, not pausing to make the inquiring inspection that may prove fatal, and to buck a predator off its back. Sudden movements and sharply raised voices will startle a young horse, and the good horseman is gentle and quiet in all his movements. Carrying a rider is a grotesque outrage of all a horses instincts

Mares usually bear a single foal. Twins are exceptional in horses. The young stay with their mothers until they are about six months old.

for self-preservation. A wild range horse, saddled and ridden for the first time with little if any preparation for the nervous shock of the terrifying weight which in the natural state would likely be that of a mountain lion or other big cat, puts up a frenzied display of desperate bucking and jumping that movie audiences throughout the world associate with bucking broncos.

The more usual method of training, which wise old horsemen often like to refer to as "gentling" rather than "breaking" the animal, involves a slow process which begins with lightly girthing a strap round the horse's middle, tightening the girth gradually as the horse becomes accustomed to moving with the unfamiliar restriction and comes to know that it will not harm him. Later a saddle is substituted, again girthed only to the point where it will hold in place; then the horseman slowly lies across the horse's back in a gradual easing of weight from leaning *against* to leaning *upon* and taking the feet off the ground so that the whole weight of the man is taken by the horse, easing a leg over to sit upright, always talking soothingly and always with another person at the horse's head. Next the horse can be lead away slowly, so that it adapts to the shifting weigh at different gaits. After schooling on gradually over one year or many the horse acquires the degree of sophistication needed of it—which will obviously be much more elementary in a pony for a young child, which needs only to be kind and quiet and sensible in traffic, than in a dressage horse or show jumper whose advanced training program takes several years to carry out. One might marvel at the superficial precocity of the racehorse, who appears on a public track a year or two before most horses are even ridden, were it not that the flat racehorse is required to do only one thing: to carry a lightweight man at a gallop, without much regard to brakes or steering. Many of these horses are not taught properly to walk or trot, are not "mouthed" in the way that makes a pleasing riding horse accept the bit, never learn to stand up on ploughed land, negotiate a fence, or stand at ease on tarmac in a busy city. Racehorses, crammed full of high protein food from weaning, so that their physical development accelerates more rapidly than that of their less valuable relations, and handled with intense attention from the moment of birth, are bred in most cases to prove their ability on the racetrack at the earliest possible moment. Having done so they spend the 16-20 years of their mature life at stud, where the value of an outstanding winner and proven sire amounts to millions of dollars.

It is for this reason that the likes of Topaz, for example, visit a stallion rather than risk taking him to the mare when she might be out of heat while other mares come ready for his services.

It is because of the value of the stallion that the normal courtship display in which a wild horse singles out a mare and pays attention to her for the brief few hours that would put her in the mood to want him is omitted—hours in which she might kick or bite him until he wins her over to his need. Because the stallion is so valuable that no damage can be risked to him, mares have their hind shoes removed and are fitted with felt boots that take the zest out of a kick, and every possible care is taken to avoid harm to either horse. The racehorse mare is first tested by a "teaser"—a stallion of no value who will win her through the early, grumpy, proud displays of pseud disinterestedness and then she is presented to the stallion who is expected to cover her across a padded board.

When the brief how-do-you-do is over and the stallion shows signs of arousal she is held by two men with a foreleg lifted off the ground so that she cannot kick out when he mounts her. After she has been covered, stallion and mare are led quickly away from each other so that no opportunity for harm occurs. Then she waits again, 11 months, fat-fed on good pasture and dried food, until once again the moment arrives for the foal of a Derby winner to take its first breath and for life to begin all over again in a horse.

Horse Sense

I am that merry wanderer of the night,
I jest to Oberon, and make him smile
When I a fat and bean-fed horse beguile,
Neighing in likeness of a filly foal.
  William Shakespeare:
  A Midsummer-Night's Dream

Horses communicate with each other and with man by a variety
of different signals which can be interpreted by such elementary
phrases as "Who are you?" "Welcome," "Is anyone around?" "I am
afraid," "I absolutely will not," "Don't go away," "I need you,"
"I am king," "Let's play." The messages are passed not just by the
sound the horse makes but by his physical stance, his air and manner,
at the moment of delivery. Many messages are purely visual:
ears cocked forwards can be taken as "I am interested," "I am happy,"
"Welcome," "What on earth is that?" depending on the circumstances
at the time. Ears laid back flat mean "I hate you," "Go away,
or I will do you harm," "I won't," or laid half back may signal
simply "I am bored," "I am thinking about something else,"
"I am dozing off."

A horse whose attention is caught by a sudden interest pricks up not just his ears but his head, focussing his whole attention on the object that attracts him. If nervous or unsure, his body tenses into a quivering alertness to run away if need be, and if very worried indeed he sweats in light patches on the neck, behind the ears and between the hind legs. His nostrils flare to their fullest extent to pick up any scents that may help him analyze what worries him, and his breath comes in short, audible snorts that communicate his fear to any horse within earshot.

Comfort from horse to horse is expressed in the mutual scratching of each other's backs and necks with a gentle rhythm of the teeth; reassurance by a head laid across the other horse's neck or by a comforting whickering of the breath. Horses are herd animals, dependent on the company of their own kind to an extent where they become uncertain, lonely and unhappy when pastured by themselves. The main line of communication, the voice, ranges from the carrying whinny of loneliness, through the short, sharp squeal of anger that usually precedes a kick, to the contented, hummering whicker of a mare encouraging her foal.

No matter what action a horse is about to take, he can be absolutely relied upon to signal his intention in advance in a recognizable, time-honored horse form. Other horses depend upon these signals for their information, and so does the observant horseman who wants to stay on board.

Talking to horses, beyond the constant soothing mutter of the horseman, begins with the horse "How do you do?" of blowing into each other's nostrils. How far the horseman wants to take it on from there is between him and his horse.

Breathing into each other's nostrils is the horse way of greeting and mutual scratching a common gesture of comfort. An arm across its neck will reassure a horse for it will feel like another horse's gesture.

Small, Vigorous and Lively

Ponies range from the maximum permitted height of 14.2 hands (58 inches) high—beyond which magic size, their build and disposition notwithstanding, they are for some reason unknown to me automatically called horses—down to the tiny Falabella breed of Argentina, which stands less than 7 hands (28 inches) at the withers. Their brains seem often in inverse ratio to their size, and the strength of their comparatively tiny bodies as well as the wide range of their intelligence has caused many generations of humans to marvel that so much complex ability should dwell in so small a compass of a horse.

A traveler to the far north of the British Isles, the Reverend John Brand, was certainly not the first to be struck by the aptitude of the Shetland pony which is indigenous to the Islands of Shetland and the Outer Hebrides; but this account of the breed, taken from his *Brief Description of Orkney, Zetland, Pightland-Firth and Caithness* and written in 1701, sums up some of the surprise that many of us have felt when first coming to know a pony: "They have a sort of little Horses called Shelties, than which

no other are to be had, if not brought thither, from other places, they are of less size than the Orkney Horses, for some will be but 9 or 10 Nevis or Handbreaths high, and they will be thought big horses there if eleven, and although so small yet are they full of vigour and life, and some not so high as others often prove to be the strongest, yea there are some, whom an able man can lift up in his arms, yet will they carry him and a woman behind him 8 miles forward and as many back; Summer or Winter they never come into an House but run upon the Mountains in some places as flocks, and if any time in Winter the storm be so great, that they are straightened for food, they will come down from the Hills when the Ebb is in the sea, and eat the Sea-Ware (as likewise do the sheep). They will live till a considerable age as 26, 28 or 30 years, and they will be good riding Horses in 24 especially they'll be more vigorous and live the longer if they be 4 years old before they are put to work . . .

"The Coldness of the Air, the Barrenness of the Mountains on which they feed and their hard usage may occasion to keep them so little,

The pupil tries to lead the teacher: at this stage the pony is usually wiser than the child.

for if bigger Horses be brought into the Country, their kind within a little time will degenerate; and indeed in the present case we may see the Wisdome of Providence, for their way being deep and Mossie in many places, these lighter Horses come through when the greater and heavier would sink down; and they leap over ditches very nimbly, yea up and down Mossy braes and Hillocks with heavy riders upon them, which I could not look upon but with Admiration, yea I have seen them climb up braes upon their knees, when otherwise they could not get the height overcome. so that our Horses would be but little if at all serviceable there."

Being by and large less valuable than horses, ponies have had a far greater chance to develop in the wild by natural selection, and consequently the native breeds of pony which inhabit practically every country are hardy in the extreme. The huge, shaggy winter coats that turn cold climate ponies into animals that would make a sheep feel under-dressed protect them against all weathers. They are far healthier living out, given a windbreak of some kind, than sweating it out in a stuffy stable. They are also instinctively greedy. Generations of plucking a living off the poor land to which so many in the past were banished when man chose the richer soils to farm has caused them automatically to put their heads down when there is anything edible at foot. For this reason a pony pastured on rich grass needs constant watching because it will stuff itself to the point where its body weight becomes more than its feet will bear and serious lamenesses, such as laminitis, will occur. A common and poignant roadside sight is that of a pony, hopelessly outclassing its child passenger, with its head stuck greedily down into a hedgerow and its rider tugging futilely at the reins.

In the past, before the industrial revolution changed the order of agriculture and the motor engine replaced the horse as common transport, ponies were used for a variety of different purposes throughout Europe and Asia. The hardy Fjord pony of Norway, one of the few breeds to have kept its identity recognizably throughout the centuries, has changed little from the horse the Vikings bred and used for horse-fights. Today it endures as a work horse in areas that are too steep or too cold for a tractor or a lorry, though its attractions as a weight-carrying riding pony have caused large numbers to be exported. The Danes, especially, are fond of it and breed it widely.

The Austrian Haflinger, a long-lived, tireless and surefooted breed, has for centuries made its living doing pack work in the high mountain passes of the Tirol. Being of a docile disposition, it has also worked

A variety of European ponies.
Top: New Forest ponies at a sale.
Above: Dales ponies at a stud in northern England.
Right: Hafflinger in Switzerland.
Top right: Welsh Mountain ponies in their natural habitat.
Far right: New Forest ponies.

Iceland ponies.

well between the shafts; and it is still occasionally so used today, though it is more common as a riding animal.

The immensely frugal Mongolian pony survives on next to nothing in the way of food. It is one of the most antique of pony types and also one of the few breeds of pony still used mainly as a working animal. It is bred in large numbers by the nomadic tribes of Mongolia, Tibet and China, and is used for herding, riding, carting, in agriculture, and for pack work. It further provides meat and milk for its masters: for the first three months after foaling the mares are regularly milked and the milk is made into cheese or fermented into *kumiss,* an alcoholic drink, on equine dairy farms. It is thought that yogurt was a Mongol invention made originally from mares' milk.

The British Isles has developed a surprisingly large number of pony breeds for its small area. The Dales pony is a strongly-built riding or cart pony which for many years carried the local doctor on his rounds. Like its slightly smaller close-relation, the Fell, its survival in quantity in modern times is largely due to its suitability as a trekking pony in the high moorlands of northern Yorkshire. The tiny Welsh Mountain pony is strong and spirited enough, although only about 12 hands high, to carry a farmer hunting all day; while the even smaller Shetland, which so surprised the Reverend Brand, was widely used down the coalmines of northern England and, when well-matched, was sometimes seen between the shafts of ladies' phaetons.

But the working uses of the past are largely disappearing. Today, the pony has become the doormat of the future equestrian, its first function being that of teaching young humans how to ride. For this it is ideally suited once the first few years of its own perilous surprise at the world has been overcome. A pony of three years old is far superior in brain power and experience to a child of the same age, and it is not until both have reached the age of nine or ten that the mental levels equal out and the child begins to have control of who goes where, and why.

Ponies are first class teachers for a young rider. For the very young and squeaky, the older the pony is the better it will put up with the frightening, frightened demands of the pupil on its back, though very old ponies are not all that keen on carrying out the wishes of the more advanced who want to hunt all day. They are quite capable of turning round and going home before the rider has had half the fun he wants. Ponies' homing instincts are extraordinary, exemplified as much in the hunting pony who, when tired, will take you home by the shortest route from any point of the compass if you loose the reins on its neck as in the renowned

Iceland pony who will carry a visitor to any destination and, turned free, will come home of its own accord within a very short period of time.

Apart from the simple ability to ride a horse—an enthusiasm that may not necessarily continue into adulthood—ponies teach children a host of things that are useful to them in later life. More than any other animal or any other form of sport, owning a pony can teach a child patience, discipline, responsibility, courage, tact, and respect for another species. A pony needs two or three hours a day of attention, at regular times of the day and in all weathers (in cases where this responsibility was not made clear before the pony was bought, many a parent has had cause to regret ever having made the purchase).

Maintenance such as daily exercise and foot care, brushing over to keep the coat attractive (deep grooming in the grass-kept pony is unadvisable, as it removes essential oils and dust which protect the animal against rough weather), regular feeding when snow covers the ground, when the pasture is too sparse to support the animal, or when hard work such as hunting is being asked of it is all fairly obvious to the casual eye. Other things that are often not taken account of when a person first thinks of purchasing a pony include the cleaning and repair of harness, routine searching of the pasture and surrounding hedges to remove poisonous plants, repairing broken fencing, providing windbreaks where necessary and maybe building a shelter of some kind so that hay can be economically fed (if simply scattered on the ground the pony will trample it, and in wet weather much of it will become soggy and unpalatable).

If all this sounds like a lot of work—well, so it is; but almost all of it is enormous fun. The miserable hours spent trailing round a field trying to catch a pony who isn't in the mood for it are made up for when the pony comes to meet you at the gate. Incidentally, it is more likely to do this if it is caught up at the same time every day, since ponies, like horses, are creatures of routine.

Right: Ponies in the Mongolian winter.
Below: Fell pony stallion.
Below right: Norwegian Fjord foal.

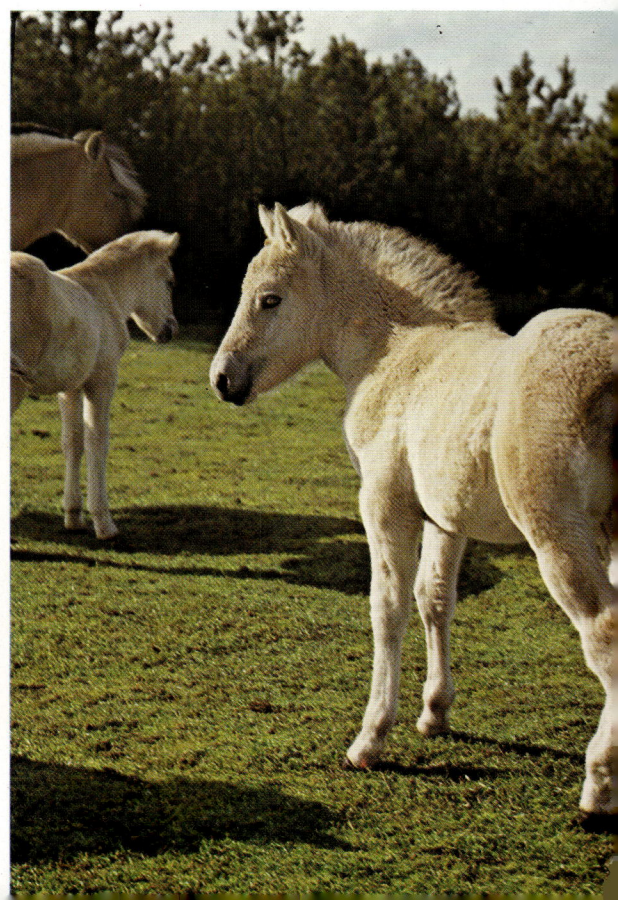

24

The thrill of padding along behind a pack of hounds, feeling a
bit proud to be there and a bit apprehensive in case you commit
some awful social bunder such as getting in front of the Master;
the soft summer evening rides after school is finished; the triumph
of your first rosette in a local gymkhana; the warm comfort
of curling into a pony's neck when everything in life seems to have
gone rotten; the friendly welcoming whicker and sweet, steaming
breath of a hungry pony on a frosty night—these things, and many
like them, are what make owning a pony special.

Ponies have a look in their eyes that is both kind and wise,
fur that turns the favourite teddy bear back into the stuffed toy
it really is, a friendly solidarity of body that strengthens and reassures,
and an ability to move with speed and grace across country
that gives you a feel of the freedom of clouds chasing each other
across the moon. They are the first true friends of many children,
a permanent anchor in a changing, growing world.

Pony events at shows. Gymkhanas provide
excellent training for young riders, offering
a variety of events calling for dexterity in
horsemanship.
Left: The sack race calls for mounting and
dismounting at speed.
Below left: Musical poles requires a controlled
canter round the outside of the ring with,
when the music stops, a quick turn and
dash for the pole, ending with an abrupt halt
from full gallop.
Below: The magnificent four-in-hand of
Shetlands, a more sedentary use of the pony
than gymkhana games, requires an adult skill
in driving.

A Matter of Forgery

Farriery is one of the oldest trades in the world still to be practised today in a form that is not so very far from the original. The abundance of blacksmiths who must have worked in villages throughout Europe during the Middle Ages can be guessed at from the enormous quantity of people surnamed Smith or Schmidt, so great that trying to pin one down in a telephone directory in any European or North American city if you have only a vague idea of his street address is a waste of time.

Not so long ago, not so far back in recent history that most adults cannot remember having seen them, nearly every village had its resident blacksmith. The forge building with its permanent coke fire always kept red-hot just under the surface, the bellows waiting to blow it into life, the familiar heavy anvil and often a line of horses quietly waiting to be shod was part of country life. After the Second World War the increasing disappearance of the farm horse in favor of the tractor led to the increasing disappearance of the smith. Many sustained themselves for a time by sideline jobs such as the working of wrought iron, but gradually smithy after smithy closed down and the farrier seemed to have departed, an important part of a vanishing past.

The smith, in fact, did not so much vanish as metamorphose. With the growing interest in riding and the boom in horse breeding that occurred in the affluent sixties, the farrier reappeared in a traveling van, driving from stable to stable upon request— all modernized, with horseshoe sizes graded in numbers just like

human shoes. Shoeing a horse cold became the done thing; though hot shoeing, which ensures a better fit, is still practised whenever possible.

A horse needs shoes to protect the working surfaces of his feet against excessive wear, the more especially so if he is used on metaled roads. The horseshoes, usually made of iron, last from four to eight weeks depending upon the amount of roadwork the horse does. During that time—generally after four weeks, but it varies with the horse—they will need removing and replacing so that the constantly-growing wall of the hoof can be pared down. If the wall of the hoof was allowed to grow out over the shoe, the tendency would be for it to split up the sides, cracking too near to the sensitive interior of the foot.

Racing shoes, called racing plates, are a different matter altogether. Aimed at giving the horse the least amount of weight to carry during a race, they are made of aluminum. Racehorses are usually "plated" the night before or upon the morning of a race, and have their work shoes replaced within a day or two because aluminum has very little durability on tarmac.

As well as making and fitting horseshoes, the skilled farrier will perform tasks requiring judgement and intelligence, such as shoeing a young horse with a shoe built up to one side to correct a bend in the leg or a faulty action.

What the old truism "a horse is only as good as its feet" really means is that a horse is only as good as the man that shoes it.

Left: Turning a hot shoe on the anvil.
Center: Trying a shoe for fit before the final alterations are made.
Above: Trimming excess nail ends from the wall of the hoof.
Right: Cold shoeing on a farm.

Natural to Man

On a clear day, when you can see forever, there usually isn't much scent about. The smell of a fox lies best on wet earth; holding earth which doesn't dry out in the sun or the wind; damp earth under a lowering sky, on a day when the pungent smells of moss and bracken steam fragrant from the hedgerows and a fine mist hangs over ponds and puddles. On such a day in any country in the temperate zone, when you hear the huntsman calling up his hounds, the occasional short, sweet blast of the horn, the deep, incessant dog-talk of his voice and the throaty answer of the excited pack; on days like this, clattering along a country road with your horse sweating up ever so slightly with anticipation, his ears pricked, his heart as high as yours, on such a day you know you're on a winner. Riding to hounds, as the expression goes (rather than riding "at" hounds, or "through" them; the last of which will probably get you sent home for bad behavior, satisfies a variety of different instincts in many men. There is the pleasure of watching a pack of hounds working a line; the thrill of a challenging fence on a good galloping horse; the independence of going off alone, judging the course the fox will take from the direction of the wind, the lie of the land, and your own intimate knowledge of the countryside (this is called "taking your own line," and your knowledge of the country had indeed better be intimate or the hunt will perform that well-known queer manoeuvre by which a half-hundred dogs, horses and people are swallowed into a landscape without trace or sound). After, there is the peace of the hot bath, the pleasure of the well-exercised body that has been tested and come through the sharpened appetite for supper and the deep release of sleep. For one reason or another most people prefer foxhunting or

staghunting. For myself, the choice falls with draghunting, a relatively minor sport in which hounds pursue a strong man-laid scent over a predetermined line with artificially-built fences. The attraction of draghunting, with its obvious limitations, is a horseman's joy in getting around the course, finishing over a 10-12 mile point with as many fences as are in the Grand National. A good drag line, being fast and guaranteed, usually requires the sort of hunter used in the "best" hunting country—the well-drained, well-fenced open grass that dominates the landscape hunted by such famous packs as Ireland's Galway Blazers, England's Quorn, or the great, timber-fenced, bold country of Maryland and West Virginia. For this, a near-bred blood horse is the sort of animal best suited; but a "hunter" may be any sort of animal, a good one being a horse that can act on the available going, whether it is the deep alluvial plough of East Anglia or the trappy, hilly country hunted by the sporting Welsh farmer packs.

After draghunting, I am inclined to rate cubhunting next for pleasure, though of an entirely different sort. Cubhunting, in which young hounds are taught their job on young foxes, precedes the season proper by some two or three months. It begins in late August or early September, starting early in the morning before the sun has burned the dew off the grass and the scent has vanished in a steam of early autumn mist, and involves those few riders who turn up to stand around a covert and turn the cub back rather than let him loose to run a line.

Cubhunting could be rather boring were it not for the quality of early morning light, the long shadows cast by a rising sun in a new day, the curious, mellow scent of autumn in the air. Getting up before the first light marks a horizon in the sky, going out in the dark to rouse a hunter blinking sleepy in a stable under the sharp, electric light; saddling up and clopping off into a gradually increasing lightness, the cobwebs on the hedgerows etched in dew: these things are part of hunting, and hunting, as Surtees' famous Mr. Jorrocks said, is natural to man.

Galloping Mania

Most European countries go in for amateur racing of one sort or another. Germany and France are notable for it, rivaling each other in the number of flat races, hurdle races and steeplechases open to the non-professional rider. Great Britain and Ireland go one step further (or may be it is one step back) by staging point-to-points, which are fund-raising hunt steeplechases limited to hunt subscribers and to horses which have been "regularly and fairly hunted". This last requirement is often a bit of polite baloney, because good hunters mostly wouldn't succeed on a steeplechase course and good chasers would be useless in the hunting field. The thrill of riding in a race for the first time, no matter whether as amateur or professional, must be much the same for all, and I suspect that the following personal account of a first ride in a race is fairly universal.

Competition for a ride in a point-to-point is very keen, and for the non-horse-owner with no previous experience of racing the chances of being offered a mount are about as thin as a cockerel's eyelash. Thus it was not until I was 30 that, by means of unscrupulous pulling of strings, I managed at last to get it set up. The horse, which was called Poorernie, belonged to a Mr. Bert Doggrell and was entered to run in a three-mile race with 18 fences at the back end of the season. I was told that Poorernie was a safe ride and experienced, which was just as well since either horse or jockey should have some knowledge of the job, and I refused Mr. Doggrel's kind offer to let me school it over fences in cold blood in case I fell off it. In February and March I went to all the local point-to-points, where I saw several nasty accidents and two horses so badly injured that they had to be shot. I learned that in these races riders sometimes fall off from exhaustion; that horses often fall through tiredness; that experienced point-to-point riders expect one accident in every 10 rides.

I knew that I had to spend the next two months in training. Getting fit took two hours a day on a racehorse (for the development of general riding muscles); 25 minutes daily with a skipping rope (lungs); 25 minutes of push-ups and lifting weights (for arm and back muscles needed on a strong horse); and two miles a day

Summer racing at
Bad Harzburg, West Germany.

of running, or alternatively sprinting and jogging (lungs again).
May came around at last, blossoming with a flippant insouciance
that I was much too terrified to share. I gathered up my hired
racing clothes and jangling nerves and drove to Larkhill, where the
meeting was, to stay the night before the race. It was a wet evening
when I arrived; on the top of Salisbury Plain the fences stood out
big and black against a grey, wind-tossed sky. Away in the distance
where the course went out of sight were clumps of newly-leafed trees
and a group of pines. In a flurry of May rain I began to walk
the course, inspecting each fence as I went.

The Larkhill course, unlike many point-to-point courses which
run over open farming land, was fenced on both sides and was used
only for racing. It was beautifully kept, with 13 neat birch stick
fences banked with gorse on the take-off side, and the course
secretary told me that £400 a year was spent on maintaining
these fences alone.

Competitors had to race round the course one and a third times
to cover the full distance of 3 miles 228 yards. The finishing post
was at the south-east end of the course, with the start a mile away
to the north-west so that the runners passed the crowd at the finish
on their first circuit, went away to the right into the country,
and came back past the start to jump the first five fences over again.
Fences 3 and 11 were open ditches—a dry ditch in front of the usual
fence—and since fence 3 was also fence 16 one had to jump
three open ditches in a race. At the far end of the course, between
the twelfth and thirteenth fences, the ground sloped sharply downhill
on a right-angled bend where I thought a horse going too fast
might easily slip, and then there was a long, slow uphill pull over
the thirteenth fence back past the start. Any horse left behind
on the hill might be too tired after the uphill pull to make up
the ground again back on the flat.

The following day I met the owner at the declaration tent. He was
calm and cheerful and had the tact not to ask if I had ridden in
a race before. This was a question I had been avoiding. He filled out
the declaration form, which is a formal announcement that a horse
will run, and handed me over to his son, Michael, for instructions
about how to ride the race. Michael told me Poorernie would judge
the jumps himself but that I must push him to keep up with the
leaders throughout. He said that at the top of the hill, passing
the start for the second time, I must move up and take the lead and
kick Poorernie on.

We went to look at Poorernie waiting in his horsebox. I had not seen
the horse before and could not see much now as most of him
was hidden under blankets, but there was an amiable chestnut face
and longish teeth, a shiny firm neck. I found out that Poorernie
had belonged to the Doggrells since he was a yearling 12 years before,
and that he was rather a family pet.

I had to change and weigh out. I was to wear Mr. Doggrell's
gold cap and black jersey, with gold hoops and blue sleeves, and
a hunting stock tight round my neck for support if I fell. In the ladies'
changing room I met the four other riders, including young
Mrs. Alderton who was down to ride a horse called Gay Quadrille,
a combination that had won me money many times before at
point-to-points.

Dressed, we went separately to weigh out, stepping on the scales
with our saddles and weightcloths. Michael handed me his
14 lb-saddle, then 7 lbs in weights (ladies must all ride at 154 lbs)
and the Clerk of the Scales nodded "OK." Then there was nothing
to do but hang around discreetly—I was told it was bad form to go
and look at the betting once you were dressed in colors—until
it was time to go into the paddock.

When Michael called me I followed numbly into the paddock.
The other owners and riders were already there, with the horses
circling round in front of a tight-packed crowd. The bell to mount

After the race is over there is the weary journey home in the horsebox,
usually unloading in the dark. Tired muscles relax with a warm
bran mash in the loosebox overnight, and by the following morning
the horse has often stiffened up. If the weather is good the horse
may be loosed for a short period in a paddock to ease his body.
Given this opportunity, almost all horses will opt for a roll, grinding
the tight, itchy bits of skin on back and sides into the rough winter grass.

sounded, and I had just a glance at my horse before I got on him.
Poorernie looked splendid, a gleaming chestnut with the muscles
standing out tight under his silken coat. He seemed at the peak
of condition for a race. Michael gave me a leg up and I was led off
round the paddock and out on to the course. As we left someone
called out to me, "Has anyone told you Gay Quadrille jumps
across to the left?"

I had the reins short and crossed on Poorernie's neck in case
the horse wanted to gallop off too fast, but as we broke into a canter
I was glad to find that, while nicely on the bit, he didn't take much
hold at all. He had a lovely stride, a very comfortable horse
going well up into his bridle, and the manners of a perfect gentleman.
A few drops of rain had fallen on us in the paddock but now
the sun was shining on the lush May grass. I cantered down to the
start feeling fine and clear-headed, Poorernie's ears pricking with
pleasure and his muscles moving rhythmically beneath his golden coat.
We walked to the first fence and looked at it together; I patted
his firm neck and spoke to him. Then we trotted back to the start,
joining the other riders who were walking in a circle behind
the Starter.

The Starter called us into line—I was second from the inside,
with Gay Quadrille on the extreme left because Mrs. Alderton
sportingly didn't want him in a position to jump across another horse
—and we all broke into a trot as we came up level with the
white flag. It fell and we were off at a gallop, Lady Allison, a gray,
leading from Gay Quadrille, Red Trawler, then me.

It happened very fast—one moment we were trotting into the start and the next we were racing at the first fence (my first dilemma: the horse needed a clear view to judge the fence correctly, whereas I needed not to see the huge thing looming up). I let Poorernie alone to see how he would take it. We were on the fence in a flash and he left the ground so early that I, accustomed to indifferent jumpers, wasn't really ready and was lucky to stay on. He flew over the fence in a huge, smooth leap, making up ground in the air. It watched the second fence and the first open ditch come up and disappear beneath us, and between the third and fourth fences

we went past Red Trawler and pushed on after Lady Allison and Gay Quadrille, who seemed to be going impossibly fast.

We came round the bend to the fifth fence on the inside, me kicking Poorernie to keep up with the leaders, flew over the straight in front of the crowd, over the sixth, and swung away into the country right-handed to meet the seventh. At our 30 m.p.h. speed the wind felt strong in our faces and our lungs were working overtime to meet a fence every 18 seconds. Gay Quadrille and Lady Allison were still in front of me, Gay Quadrille jumping well clear to the left and me on the inside following Poorernie's inclination to keep tight on the bends.

Poorernie was the perfect horse, sensible, talented and enjoying himself, and he seemed also to know the Larkhill course very well. We swallowed up the seventh fence, and at the eighth the leaders were only two lengths clear of us and I had a searing pain in my lungs. Round the S-bend between the eighth and ninth we flashed through bright gorse, the gray Lady Allison three lengths in the lead and Gay Quadrille's muscular bay quarters about a length ahead of us. Poorernie was going superbly, jumping straight with never a mistake and still cutting all the corners.

Over the twelfth Lady Allison still had a three-length lead over Gay Quadrille, who was a little ahead of me but now in touch. Then downhill to the slippery right-angled bend, and Lady Allison nose-dived on the wet grass and almost sat down: I shouted out something fatuous like, "Well sat," to her rider, who was magnificently still in the saddle, and she called back with something equally neurotic which sounded like, "Don't let that old b . . . . jump across me," and we shot past on the inside.

At the long climb up there was only Gay Quadrille in front of us, and for the first time it occurred to me that we might win.

Ladies suffer from racing nerves just as badly as the men. In many countries, because of the severely limited opportunities for women to race, the tension of the inexperienced jockey is visible at the start of the race, as can be seen in the picture above. It's allright once you get settled down (right), but the first few seconds of a race can be horrific. Connoisseurs of the art of swearing are advised to stand by the first fence in any ladies' point-to-point and listen: it is one of the surest venues in the world for a guaranteed demonstration of rough language.

I gave Poorernie an extra shove with the legs. He moved straight up level with Gay Quadrille at the thirteenth fence; we came over the top of the hill together back in sight of the crowd and raced neck-and-neck for the next four fences. There was a great sense of aloneness and exhilaration—the horses behind us were lost in the rushing wind and I was aware of a peculiar mixture of sensations. The thudding of our flight. Sun. A lark's song borne back towards us. Poorernie's straining muscles. The fences rising up at us and flashing by underneath like breaking waves. Exhaustion. At the sixteenth fence, the open ditch again, Mrs. Alderton and I were six lengths clear, and, I believe, having some sort of silly chat about how to get fit. At the seventeenth, with only the right-hand bend and one fence left before the winning post, Gay Quadrille jumped left as usual and this time simply disappeared out of my field of vision. Turning to the right with Poorernie hugging the rails I had the extraordinary sight of no one in front. Just one jump to go and a noise coming up from the crowd; I felt very much alone. Now there was only me and Poorernie with his game pricked ears and his clever feet.

I pushed him a bit with what strength remained and we were over the last. Still 200 yards from the finish, Poorernie slowed down, seemed to lose momentum. I hit him lightly down the shoulder and called out to him, and he leaped forward with a fine burst of speed to the post.

At first I thought only: we've got where we had to go. Poorernie knew it too and pulled himself up without help from me. Other members of the field, still galloping, went past us; and in my stupor I envied them because they had been riding in a point-to-point. Finally it hit me that we had won. Gay Quadrille was second, Lady Allison third.

Then Poorernie turned himself around and headed for the winners' enclosure, and Michael Doggrell came up and said I must take the saddle off myself so that no one could be thought to have tampered with the weights, and must take the saddle and the weight cloth and weigh in—which I did, at 5 lbs lighter than before the race. I told Bert Doggrell that I hadn't ridden in a point-to-point before, and he said that was all right because he hadn't told me that the horse had never been raced by a woman before and that the last time Poorernie had run at Larkhill he had fallen at the second open ditch. So we laughed, and had champagne.

Above: Racing at Frankfurt. *Left:* Hurdle racing. A fall over a small fence can be just as nasty as a fall over a big one. But one man's disaster can clear a nice gap for the horses following behind—always provided that the faller does not trip them up.

They're off

In winter, the first lot goes out with the first light, stirred out of sleep by the bustle of the stable lads and the strong, authoritative voices of the trainer and head lad. Usually it's all a bit of a rush, a sharp change from dozing in a warm straw bed to the cold bit in the mouth as the bridle is lifted up over the ears. The overnight rugs come off and are piled into a corner, the saddle is girthed in place and a work blanket is fastened neatly over the top to keep the frost from getting at the thin, silk hide. Mane and tail are brushed in place, the hooves picked out, and the racehorse is led out into the sharp, exhilarating blast of morning, bucking and kicking with excitement under his featherweight exercise boy.

When they are all assembled in the stable yard they go out on to the racetrack, the exercise grounds, the downs, or indoor school, depending on the country and the weather. The colts go first and then the geldings, the fillies trailing off behind to keep their scent from getting to the young stallions up in front. Youth, high protein, and the morning wind stir up their blood so that even a rustle in the dead, dry grass will take them wheel away, whip round, rear up, kick out; and if they drop their riders, off they go, floating with easy grace along the track or turning in towards the string to make the other horses jump and kick and play. Mostly at this time of year they only walk and trot, because (except in sub-tropical regions such as Florida and southern California) there isn't any flat racing until the spring comes in and so there is no call to be hard fit. Steeplechasers, though, being in the middle of their racing season, come up the gallops one by one, moving at a steady half-speed gallop with perhaps ten lengths between each horse.

When the hour-long exercise is done the lads dismount and lead

Morning exercise on Newmarket Heath, greatest of the British training grounds. In the first light, at a walk, all horses are potential winners and all stable boys potential jockeys. But, though they serve the full five years of their apprenticeship, very few of these lads will ever see a racecourse except on foot.

Ploughed gallops (*below* and *far right*) are strips of gravel deeply turned and raked. Steady work on the plough, with each foot sinking in to fetlock-deep, builds muscle on the horse more quickly than the easier travel over grassland (*center*).

the last mile home to ease their horses' backs. Shut up in their looseboxes again the horses get the sweat and mud cleaned off them, their hooves picked free of stones and dirt, their coats brushed over and, if wet, dried off. Then the indoor rugs are buckled into place, the hayrack filled, fresh water brought, and finally a rich, sweet breakfast feed is poured into the mangers and the horses are left in peace to eat and sleep until the time arrives for evening stables.

After the lads themselves have breakfasted the second lot goes out. In most flat stables this will be the yearlings, accompanied by a wise old horse or two to lead them and to teach them manners. Wandering a little from side to side as they fail to get their balance quite correct, they learn to walk and trot and canter in single file,

and after that to work upsides in threes and fours. They are the unknown quantity in racing; the young, unproven, who have never seen a racetrack. On average only one out of four will ever win a race of any kind, but at this stage there is always an owner or a stable lad who thinks each horse a budding superstar.

A few of them will never see a racetrack, breaking down in wind or limb in training and may be going straight to stud. Others may become "morning glories"—horses who work well enough at home, but at the racetrack in the afternoon have lost their early morning zest. Some will prove too slow, or will be entered in the wrong races (one of the most important skills of a great trainer is to enter a horse against others that it is likely to beat, and this requires, apart from talent, an intimate knowledge of all racetracks and all other horses likely to compete). Many more are simply not competitive. Any fool can get a horse to gallop, but if the urge to win is not instinctive to it he'll never make a racehorse.

There are horses who do best at certain seasons of the year. Early runners, tearing up the racetrack in the spring, grow lazy and lose their form when the summer sun gets on their backs. Others take weeks or months to come to their peak, only really running on when the season is more than halfway over.

Within the general type called "racehorse" there are many different kinds of animal. There are sprinters, on the small side and compactly built, who can jump out of the starting stalls at a tearaway pace and maintain their speed for short distances not exceeding a mile. There are stayers who, though they cannot live with a sprinter over five or six furlongs, yet have a steady,

remorseless stride which brings them home in front over two miles or more. The most desired among the flat-race horses are those who, at three and four years old, beat the best of their age group at a mile and a half, thus showing a mixture of the sprinter's turn of foot and the stayer's strength of heart and limbs. The most valuable prizes —the American Triple Crown, the French Arc de Triomphe, and the English Derby—are designed for horses of this sort, and it is the winners of these races who later command the greatest price at stud.

Steeplechase horses, who are expected to cover long distances and jump big fences, come into their prime at about eight years old and are a somewhat different sort of thoroughbred. Although they may be bred along very similar lines to the flat horse they are slower to develop, and when they reach maturity often show greater depth and more bone. These horses must have stamina, sense and courage. At their best they compete for England's Cheltenham Gold Cup, the greatest honor in chasing; and stiffer and more widely-known trials exist for them, so dangerous that the owners of some top chasers will not permit their horses to be entered. These are the Aintree Grand National, held in northern England, and Czechoslovakia's dramatic Grand Pardubice. Both are held annually, the National in the spring and the Pardubice in the autumn, and both are run over roughly 4½ miles with 30 or so fences; though the Pardubice, which is run on both plough and grass, has, unlike the National, a variety of different sorts of fences to be jumped and is therefore more suited to the kind of horse with a leaning towards cross-country work and less to the big, bold sort of chaser

that might win the National. The world's most horrifying fence, the Taxis, occurs in the Pardubice. A natural hedge 5 feet (1.5 metres) high and 5 feet wide conceals from the approaching horse a ditch 16 foot 5 inches (5 metres) wide and 6 foot 6 inches (2 metres) deep on the landing side. Many, taken unprepared, fall into this ditch, and many more fall over the fallers.

The most popular of all types of racing, trotting, does not involve the true thoroughbred horse, although the Standardbreds of America, the Orlov and Métis Trotters of Russia, and the French and German Trotters mostly carry more thoroughbred blood in their veins then they do of any other breed. Trotting racing seems to have evolved separately in several different countries as a natural part of such activities as taking the gig to market and seeing if you could out-trot the other fellow. The craze in Germany, where trotting is twice as popular as thoroughbred racing, began in the second half of the 19th century. The first trotting club, the Altona, was formed in Hamburg in 1874, and the basis of the modern German Trotter was the Russian Orlov, 18th-century brainchild of Count Alexius Grigorievich Orlov (who may also have been the murderer of Czar Peter III). Massive doses of American Standardbred blood, so-called because each performer must achieve a minimum standard of speed over one mile before it is allowed on the racetrack, and more recently of that of the French Trotter has built the German horse into a high-calibre competitor. The German record over 1,000 metres of 1 minute 17.3 seconds is held by Permit, who is by Epilog, one of the most famous of the German Trotter sires.

Starting stalls, a modern development that is now in almost universal use (*top:* Newmarket, England; *center:* Arizona, USA; *bottom:* Germany), ensure an even break for all. From there on in factors of speed and skill soon sort them out.

Right: Passing the finishing post, Marseilles, France.

Thoroughbred racing varies from country to country, and about the only generalisation universally true of a trainer's working day is that it is never done. In the smaller European countries, horses are trained at the trainer's own establishment and are shipped out to race as they come ready, sometimes staying overnight but never away from home for more than a day or two. During the racing season, normal work for the trainer will entail getting up in time to see the first lot work, and soon after that usually having to leave for a far-away racetrack to see one of his horses run or to learn the form of other runners. It is for this reason that the horses who are most imminently ready to race go out with the first lot, and for this reason that the first lot has to be over and done with and back in the stables by about 9 o'clock in the morning.

After the first lot, if the trainer is having a rare easy day, he goes out to watch the second lot. More often he drives or takes a light aircraft to the racetrack, arriving in time to saddle his runner and to give instructions to the jockey. In the Paddock he may meet the owner of the horse, with whom he goes over the animal's probable performance, and, later, its actual performance. After racing he rushes home in time for evening stables, when his lads are cleaning and mucking out the horses, and inspects every horse in his charge. If this were not enough, there is a lot of paperwork to be done. Corn, hay and straw must be chosen and paid for; veterinary and farriers' bills debited to the right horse so that owners' accounts can be made up fairly; entries made long in advance and the forfeit stages noted; horseboxes organized and accommodation reserved for horses and lads who will stay overnight at the races. There are also written reports on the progress of horses to be made up and sent out, telephone calls to owners and time spent socially with them.

Yet, if the European trainers seem to have a hard life of it, American and Russian trainers can make them look almost indolent. Because of the vast tracts of territory involved, horses are trained on the racetracks; and trainers, having horses working at three or more tracks simultaneously, fly from place to place, living like jet-set gipsies in motels and airplanes. In America the racing season goes on relentlessly all the year round. A trainer is likely to live in Florida from January until the end of March, then move up to New York for racing at Belmont and Aqueduct in the spring. In August there is the Saratoga meeting in upper New York State. Meanwhile the trainer may be running horses in Chicago, or flying one across for a big race on the West Coast, or living temporarily at Hollywood Park. In the fall it is back to New York, and at the end of November racing begins again in Florida. All this, plus the paperwork and so on. Training racehorses is not a job but a dedicated way of life, an avocation that consumes at the expense of all other interests.

The only reason for it has to be the peculiar fascination of the racehorse. Man has been drawn to racing horses since time out of mind. The first recorded instance of a race appears on Hittite cuneiform tablets dated 4,000 years BC, and before the days when man could write it seems likely that he raced his horses against his neighbor's. Though it has since become a multi-million dollar industry, the hard core of racing remains the same: a delight beyond price in the speed and courage of a horse.

Above left: Accidents are more likely when the horse is tired. This faller is coming over the last jump on a course with a slight uphill gradient.
Top right: Very few even get to the last in the gruelling British Grand National. In this picture, taken during the 1975 race, L'Escargot (blinkered), the eventuel winner, fights it out with Red Rum, winner in '73 and '74.
But even where no fences are involved, nothing is certain to stay on its feet. A slip on the snow at St. Moritz (*left*) or a tangle of Canadian wheels in the trotting race (*center right*) or chuck wagon race (*right*) could cause a nasty pile up.

Wild Horses

This is the age when the old saw about "wild horses couldn't drag you away" has finally come true. It isn't that the wild horse has developed a bad case of cold feet; it's simply that there aren't enough wild horses around to do a proper job. The truly wild horse is near extinction, and with its passing a vanishing dream becomes a legend.

Millions of years before man began, great herds of horses roamed freely over the face of the earth. They had the wind to tell them where the water was; the knowledge, passed from horse to horse by demonstration, of the summer pastures high up in the hills. Distances meant little to them, and the migration down the mountainside when winter stung them round the ears, the haul across the plains to shelter where the snow was thin enough to scrape a living, was just a part of normal life. They ran instinctively from natural enemies, shying at logs and ditches which could conceal all manner of invader and approaching water holes with caution. Some, adapted to the scrub forests of northern Europe, were elk-like in the head and browsed off trees. Others, more like the modern horse to look at, grazed on the steppes and plains of central Asia.

Hungary: A free-range herd is brought in. The tamer headcollared pair in the center have been loosed to guide the others and to help them settle down.

Each herd was governed by a king, a stallion, proud of his mares and foals, diligent in driving off the intruder, forever on the watch against attack or danger. Often he was challenged by a rival horse, a colt or loner paying court to some of his mares, and only by strength and brainpower could a stallion maintain his herd. Gradually, and largely through the agency of man, the horse grew taller and its territory increased. Only in the last few centuries have there been horses in Australia or America, and it is largely there, to the small extent that they exist, that the truly wild horse remains. The Australian Brumby—whose name is probably derived either from a pioneer horsebreeder called James Brumby, from "baroomby," the Queensland aboriginal word for wild, or from Baramba, the name of a station and creek in Queensland— still carries on in microscopic numbers because it is almost impossible to train, and so, once caught, is scarcely worth the effort. The curious thing about the Brumby, which is now a genuine wild horse of considerable intelligence, is that it originated only just over a century ago from feral horses when the great Australian gold rush

of the mid-nineteenth century caused many domestic horses to be turned loose on the ranges to breed as they chose. They proliferated rapidly, accelerated by the redundancy of twentieth-century horses which were sent to join them when mechanisation became the thing, and since World War II have been heavily culled because of the damage they did to agricultural land, so that now very few are left. Something of the same story happened to the North American Mustang. Horses were introduced to the Americas by the Conquistadores of the fourteenth to fifteenth centuries. Those that escaped, or were let loose, quickly deteriorated on the ranges from high-quality Spanish stock into plain scrub horses which, from natural selection, became very tough and brainy. These were the ponies the Indians used, conforming to no special color, size or shape, and they were also the original cow ponies. They have been culled for agricultural reasons, shot for dog meat and for glue; and today there would be no Mustangs left were it not for government laws ensuring their protection.

Two of the original types of wild horse still exist, or just about. Both, in height, are only ponies, and both exude a ferocity unknown in the tractable domestic horse that has been a friend of man for centuries. One type, kept alive by zoos and wildlife parks and living semi-wild in a Polish herd at Popielno, is the Tarpan, an Ice Age horse which was once widespread in Europe and Asia. It formed part of the make-up of many primitive horses, and so

Left: The two oldest breeds of horse still known to man—the Tarpan (*above*) and the Asiatic Wild Horse (also called Przewalskii's Horse). Few now remain, and their survival is due largely to their interest for zoos and wildlife parks.
Below: A Brazilian remuda, semi-wild, is brought in from the ranges.

is a basic part of the ancestry of the more sophisticated modern breeds. It is a curious horse, having sometimes the striped coat that would make it invisible in the forest and occasionally turning white in winter, as Arctic animals do.

The Tarpan appears to have divided into two groups, one wandering in eastern Europe and the other grazing on the steppes of the Ukraine. It has been hunted for food for millennia; much as deer were hunted, but more ruthlessly because the Tarpan stallion would attack his domestic rival ferociously. Tarpan meat was regarded as such a great delicacy that by the end of the eighteenth century it had been hunted almost to extinction.

Left: The famous white horses of the Camargue, which run loose in the marshes of the Rhône delta and are the mounts of the local gauchos. The Camarguais, technically a pony because of its short stature, owes its fame more to its highly-photogenic surroundings than to its ability.

Above: A frightened Dülmen weanling is separated from the herd.

There is a Mongolian legend of Tarpan which concerns the Torguls, a human tribe descended from a Tarpan stallion. On the day of the birth of Torgut, son of lovely Irgit and magnificent Tarpan, stallions, mares and foals came from all points of the compass to witness the event. After a fierce fight with wolves, in which the stallions routed 20,000 of them, Tarpan, immortalized, trotted proudly away with the young prince on his back.

The other still-extant primitive wild horse, the Asiatic Wild Horse (also known as *Equus Przewalskii Przewalskii Poliakov,* or Przewalskii's Horse), still just about survives in the Tachin Schara Nuru Mountains, the Mountains of the Yellow Horses, on the western fringe of the Gobi Desert. Like the Tarpan it has been hunted to near-extinction, and its biggest chance of survival lies in European and American zoos; and like the Tarpan it is an Ice Age relic. It lives in a rigorous climate with little food of any quality, and its savage attitude to outsiders must have something to do with its continuity of form. In its wild state stallions

and even two-year-old colts will attack and kill invading males long before they get within reach of the mares, and run away domestic mares who attempt to join the band are usually insufficiently hardy to withstand the extreme conditions in which the Asiatic Wild Horse lives.

Herds of semi-wild horses still continue to endure, running loose in the great remudas (remount herds) of Russia, the Americas and eastern Europe, but most of these horses are already broken to the saddle. At the very least they have parents who are broken in, and when their own turn arrives will be rounded up and trained as needed. It is sometimes convenient to let the horses fend for themselves, but as agricuture encroaches all the time on common land the areas in which horses can run without doing damage become increasingly limited. Small private herds on large private estates, such as the Dülmen ponies which run semi-wild on a reserve in Westphalia, are becoming more the natural way of life.

On common ground throughout the world, horses and ponies will continue to roam at will—that is, until their masters catch them up and work them. But time, as well as masters, catch them up. The day of the wild horse is done, succumbing like so many independent creatures of the demands of domesticity.

The North American Mustang performs its traditional role of bucking bronco. This hasty method of breaking a wild horse by strapping a saddle on its back and sitting there until it had bucked itself into exhaustion was originally used because most working cowboys hadn't time to spare to train vast quantities of animals gently. It survives today in the sporting attraction of the rodeo bronc. The best of these have been ridden many times unsuccessfully, bucking through a powerful instinct to dislodge any rider and sometimes impelled to great jumps and pitches by a cinch strapped uncomfortably round the tender skin of their bellies.

Drinkers of the Wind

Allah said to the South Wind: "Become solid flesh, for I will make a new creature of thee, to the honour of
My Holy One, and the abasement of Mine enemies, and for a servant to them that are subject to Me."
And the South Wind said: "Lord, do Thou so."
Then Allah took a handful of the South Wind and he breathed thereon, creating the horse and saying:
"Thy name shall be Arabian, and virtue bound into the hair of thy forelock, and plunder on thy back. I have
preferred thee above all beasts of burden, inasmuch as I have made thy master thy friend. I have given thee
the power of light without wings, be it in onslaught or in retreat. I will set men on thy back, that shall honor
and praise Me and sing Hallelujah to My Name."

Bedouin legend.

The Arabian has been selectively bred for more than 1,000 years
longer than any other breed of horse, and there are those who claim
that he has run wild in the deserts of Arabia for many millennia.
Others disagree on the grounds that no prehistoric horse bones
have ever been found in the desert, and they are supported
by the fact that the Arab was not one of the twelve breeds mentioned
by the Romans; nor is there any mention of him in pre-Roman
history. The Mohammedans believed, literally, that Allah created
him out of a handful of the south wind, but very probably they were
barking up the wrong genealogical tree. A more likely source
of origin, at least in part, is the ancient race of Turkoman,
or Turkmene, horses of the steppe and desert regions of central Asia.

Selective breeding of the Arab by the Bedouin has been going on
since at least the time of Mohammed (seventh century AD),
and there is evidence to suggest that it was practised for as long as
a thousand years before that. The Bedouins' ruthless attention
to purity of line—so absolute that unless a horse was known
to be *asil* (pure) he could never be bred into the *asil* line no matter
how perfect his conformation—and the exceptional hardships

Below: Standing among the devout at prayer the holy Arab, having
brought his master to the mosque, is a natural part of the religious scene.
Right: Bedouin in Morocco. "The Evil One dare not enter into a tent
in which a pure-bred horse is kept" is an injunction in the Koran.

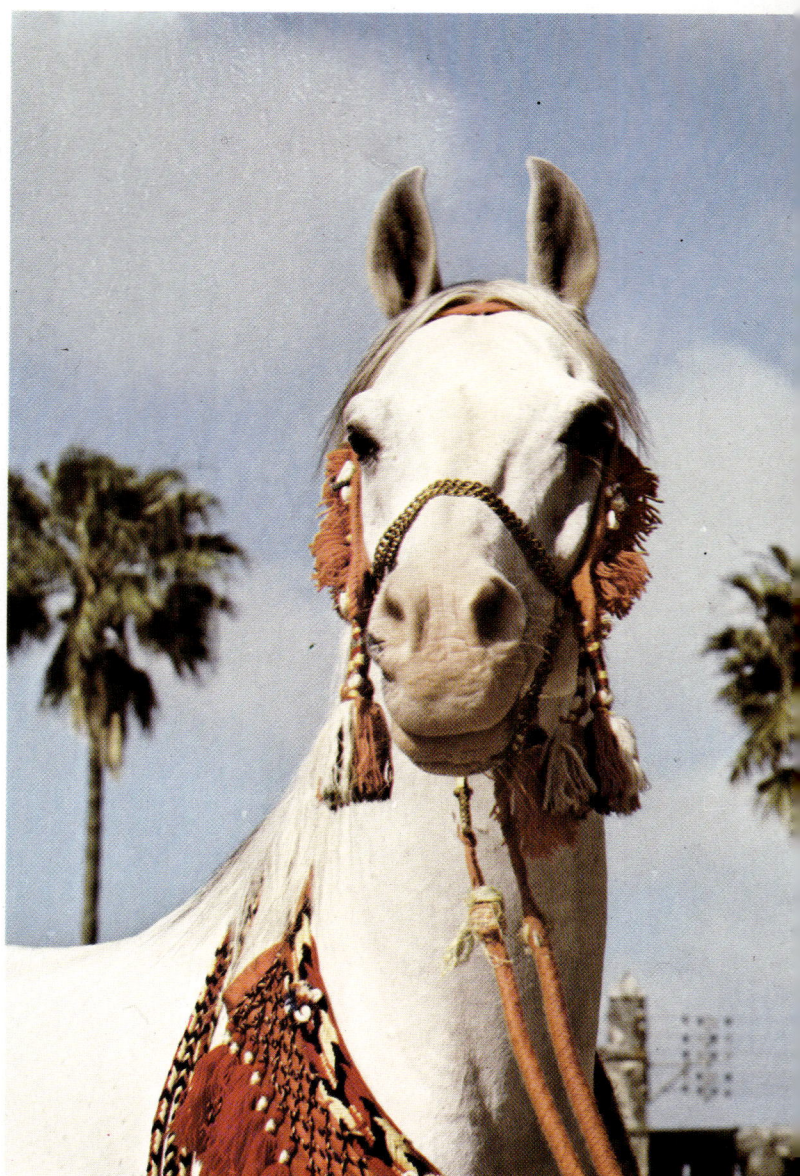

A breed of horse, though pure in blood-line, varies with the climate in which it lives and the richness of its pasture. The Polish Arabs (*above and right*) and the Moroccan Arab (*top right*) are noticeably finer-drawn than their luxuriant cousins (*top, center*) which are brought up on the deep grassland of southern England.

of the desert climate are the two factors that have produced this fine animal, the most graceful and individual horse in the world. Food was scarce in the desert. Grass grew only in winter and early spring, and for the rest of the year the horses lived off camel's milk, dried dates, locusts, and dried camel's meat. Only the strong could endure it. So convinced was Mohammed of the military importance of these tough desert horses, which he bought from the wandering tribes and paid for with human slaves, that he wrote into the Koran an irresistible injunction to men to feed their horses well: "As many grains of barley as thou givest thy horse, so many sins shall be forgiven thee."

Religious commandment reinforced by an extraordinary passion for their horses led the Bedouin into a man-to-horse relationship unequalled to this day. It was to last for thirteen centuries. Not only did a man share his food with his horse, but he even slept with it; and this, too, was on the instruction of Mohammed. (Or maybe it wasn't so much an instruction as a roundabout threat. What Mohammed put about through the agency of the Koran was this: "The Evil One dare not enter into a tent in which a pure-bred horse is kept.")

The mares, and not the stallions, were the animals most highly prized, and were the mounts that were used for war and plunder, the stallions being relegated to a role more similar to that of the

drone bee. Purity of blood line was treated with fanatical seriousness, and horses were generally inbred to reinforce good qualities—an entirely foreign concept to the Western breeder, whose school of thought has it that inbreeding produces congenital weaknesses. The several hundred "families" of the Arabian horse were divided into three main types, which are still to be seen today. They are: *Kehylan,* the masculine type, symbol of power and endurance; *Seglawi,* the feminine type, symbol of beauty and elegance, and *Munigi,* the angular type, symbol of speed and racing. The breeding of one Arabian type with another is not always desirable, since the offspring is sometimes of lesser quality than either parent.

Arabs were probably first introduced into Europe during the Moorish invasions of the western Mediterranean. Incidental breeding with local mares must have occurred, but there is little evidence to suggest that in those early times the Arab was thought of in Europe as anything more than perhaps a decorative parade mount. During the Crusades, captured Arab horses seem again to have acquired some stature as fit mounts for kings and princes on state occasions, though as cavalry chargers they never entered into consideration because the heavy armor of the times required horses of enormous size and power to carry it. Light arms and armor changed all that. From the Renaissance through the Napoleonic wars the superiority of the Turkish mounts, in fleetness of foot and movement and in endurance, was obvious, and the demand for Arab blood began to grow in Europe. Following the disastrous retreat from Moscow in the bitter winter of 1812, Napoleon's aide-de-camp wrote to his superior officer:

"The Arab horse withstood the exertions and privations better than the European horse. After the cruel campaign in Russia almost all the horses the Emperor had left were his Arabs. General Hubert . . . was only able to bring back to France one horse out of his five, and that was an Arab. Captain Simonneau, of the General Staff, had only his Arab left at the end, and so it was with me also."

Given such proofs as these, Arabians were wanted wherever courage and stamina were at a premium, and so it came about that during the Crimean War vital news of the Russian defeat was entrusted to an Arab-mounted messenger. The bay stallion Omar Pasha galloped the 93 miles from Silistra to Varna in one day. His rider fell dead of exhaustion, but Omar Pasha seemed fresh as ever . . . Arab horses are sometimes known as Drinkers of the Wind.

Above: A rare use of the Arab in Ethiopia. The Gougs Game, a contest with lances not unlike the mediaeval sport of jousting, is now seen only in remote areas. It is held in December, and contests may last several days with as many as 200 participants.

Right: The natural vitality of a young English Arab stallion.

Today the Arabian is bred in many countries, showing slight differences of type according to national preference, and variations in height and build according to the climate and the terrain (obviously a horse bred on rich temperate-zone pasture will be bigger and softer than his dry, desertbred cousin). Though his cavalry days are over, his dash and spirit as a riding horse ensure his future, and his prepotency as a sire will endure, as in so many cases in the past, wherever a new breed of quality and fire is evolved.

60

The Competitors

The origins of competitive show jumping are in all probability Irish. The earliest "leaping" contests to have been recorded were held at the Royal Dublin Society's annual horse show in 1865, where the "high leap" (three bars standing 4 feet 10 in) and the "wide leap" (a pair of parallel hurdles) were introduced as part of the test of a good hunter. Horses who had got over the high leap successfully were automatically qualified for a crack at the championship leap on the last day of the show, which was competed for over a 5 ft 10 in stone wall.

Leaping was not to be treated as a serious sport until many decades had passed, and so the records of its beginnings are woolly. It seems to have broken out fairly spontaneously in British agricultural shows of the 1870's, and to have occurred in North America at much the same time. It must have become popular in Europe soon after, as three jumping competitions were held at the Paris Olympics of 1900, two of them won by Belgium and one by France.

In 1902 a North American hunter named Heatherbloom cleared 8′ 3″ before witnesses on his owner's farm, though 7 ft 10½ in was the highest he ever managed in the show ring. Heatherbloom's 8 ft 3 in is not official in the sense that it is not recognized by the governing body of equestrian sports, the Brussels-based Fédération Equestre Internationale (hardly surprising, since the F.E.I. was not formed until 1921). The official F.E.I. records are as follows:

High jump 8 ft 3 in (2.47 m), held by Captain Alberto Larraguibel Morales of Chile, riding Huasó in a contest at Vina del Mar, Santiago, Chile on February 5th 1949;

Long jump over water 27 ft 2¾ in (8.30 m), held by Lieutenant-Colonel Lopez del Hierro of Spain, riding Amado Mió at Barcelona on July 1st 1951.

During the first half of the twentieth century show jumping was dominated by army officers. The two greatest men to influence the sport were Captain Federico Caprilli of the Italian Cavalry, who developed the forward seat in jumping and spent almost all his short life (he was killed in a fall when he was 39) studying and improving on jumping techniques, and the dedicated Colonel Paul Rodzianko of the Russian Imperial Guard, who after the Revolution became a director of the Cavalry School in Dublin and the trainer of the Irish team.

The army, which did so much for competitive show jumping between the wars, lost its grip a bit after World War II. Certainly there were many officers who still stayed in the game—recent history rings with famous names such as those of Italy's great d'Inzeo brothers, Captain Raimondo and Colonel Piero, England's Colonel Mike Ansell and Wales's Colonel Harry Llewellyn— but the civilian foot was in the stirrup and its grip is becoming stronger all the time. Most of the great international names nowadays belong to private people, a steady stream of farmers, businessmen and lady riders from countries throughout the world. Supreme

among these are the consistently-good German riders, whose brilliant international performances, both as individual and team members, make them the most formidable competitors in the world. Names such as Hartwig Steenken, Men's World Champion 1974 on his great Hanoverian mare Simona, Alwin Schockemöhle with his bold grey Rex the Robber (so all-conquering at Britain's Royal International Horse Show in 1975 that some called it "Schockemöhle's benefit week") and his almost equally famous brother, Paul Schockemöhle, tend to dominate the sport.

Show jumpers come in all shapes and heights, ranging from Marion Mould (née Coakes)'s tiny Stroller, who, though only 14.1½ hands high, won the Women's World Championship in 1965 (when his rider was only 17) and competed for the British team in the 1968 Mexico Olympics, to horses standing well over 17 hands high. Most are mongrels, though the odd ex-racehorse, Anglo-Arab or other purebred is seen from time to time. There are no hard and fast laws about show jumpers excepting one: the horse must be a natural jumper, fond of jumping and brave-hearted, usually showing early in life by the enthusiasm and spring in him that he has the aptitude and the inborn wish to clear a fence. It helps also if he is handy, quick to collect himself and sharp to turn; but these things can be taught him by a good rider. The prices paid for show jumpers are so far in excess of the money they can win in prizes that show jumping has become a rich man's hobby, or, in many cases, a sport requiring the backing of a sponsor. A green horse showing jumping potential is worth £ 4,000 and up. A top-class international performer is beyond price, though a realistic guess for someone who wants to buy one might be between £ 80,000—£ 100,000. These horses have no worth at stud, and are only valuable in terms of the pleasure they may bring to their owners.

Much the same sort of generalization applies to the event horse, though he usually contains a large proportion of thoroughbred blood because he must be fast if he is to succeed in the cross-country and steeplechase sections of the game. A top three-day eventer is an outstanding all-rounder, possessed of courage and endurance as well as versatility. He is judged on his discipline at dressage, his speed over a steeplechase course, his endurance on roads and tracks, his adaptability and bravery over a tough cross-country course, and finally on his ability over show jumps. Three-day eventing is the supreme test of discipline and guts in horse and rider, requiring years of training and hard work and the sacrifice of almost all other interests to the pursuit of perfection.

Unlike racing, eventing is open to both sexes without prejudice, and it is here that equality in equestrianism for men and women is most freely able to prove itself. In the 1975 European Three-Day Event Championships, held at Luhmühlen, West Germany, first and

Alwin Schockemöhle on his famous show jumper Rex the Robber, winner of the Grand Prix at Britain's Royal International Horse Show in 1975.

second individual places went to women riders, both British: Lucinda Prior-Palmer riding her own Be Fair, and H.R.H. The Princess Anne on Goodwill; though the team event, a compilation of the best three scores put up by four competitors named as competing for any one nation, went to the all-male Russian team.

Dressage, the supreme art form of equestrianism, is designed to improve the natural balance and movement of the horse. It is a developed form of artistry which began centuries ago with the need for manoeuvrability and unquestioned discipline in the war horse, and which has been refined into such seemingly-impossible feats

A well-designed show jumping course will test the all-round ability of horse and rider.

Top: A wide parallel needs speed and scope.

Above: A wall with pole, narrower and usually taller than a parallel, requires more vertical thrust, less forward impulsion.

Right: The great Schockemöhle and Rex the Robber move into a triple bar. The rider balances his weight so that it lies over the center of gravity of his horse.

as a controlled leap into the air from a standstill or the ability to canter backwards on three legs. From the military point of view the advantages are huge: a horse that would move sideways or backwards as readily as it would move forwards; one that would turn on its own axis, no matter whether the front or rear was used as a pivot; one that would leap over a fallen horse or rear up to confront an enemy, would move from a standing start straight into a gallop—advantages such as these makes the horse a fighting force that is far ahead of the armored car in every aspect except vulnerability.

Unfortunately, vulnerability being at a premium and hand-to-hand fighting not much the fashion any more, the horse has lost its place in warfare and dressage has been relegated to an act of love and dedication confined to those few who will give up their lives to horsemanship for the sake of itself.

The highest form of dressage, *haute école,* is that in which the horse moves freely and lightly in perfect balance, responding so directly to his rider's invisible commands that he seems to be moving of his own immaculate volition. This form of riding has been made world famous by the amazing Spanish Riding School, which was founded at Vienna some three or four centuries ago (the date of origin has never been clarified) and was called "Spanish" because the horses used by it originate from Spain. The horses of the Spanish riding school are grays of the Lipizzaner breed, taken from

Left and below: Varied obstacles, often from rising or falling ground, test all-round ability in the cross-country phase of a three-day event.

A difference in style: In the show jumping phase of eventing (*top left*), the all-round rider sits centred on a long rein over a comparatively small fence which her horse clears with the unnecessarily-big leap of the non-specialist. Tackling the big spread of a birch oxer (*above*), the experience and economy of top-class show jumping are evident in the low-slung forward seat of the rider. Though she maintains her balance to use her weight to her horse's best advantage, experience has taught her that the short distances between show jumping fences will not give her time to "slip" her reins midway in the air and shorten them again before she reaches the next fence.

The cross-country rider (*top left*) lands into the water on the typically-long rein of one who has ample time to readjust his position before the next obstacle is reached.

A show jumping rider (*left*) who has approached his obstacle more slowly lands all set to take on the next jump.

Supreme control of the horse in a fairly advanced dressage manoeuver. The rider, Josef Neckerman on Mariano, sits immobile, his signals so slight that they are not noticeable.

the former Imperial stud farm at Lipizza, founded by Archduke Charles in 1580 on Andalusian stock with perhaps a sprinkling of Barb and Arab blood. Stallions only are used in the school, and after three or four years of training learn most of the basics of *haute école,* which is also known as "airs on the ground." The really talented horse may then go on to the "airs above the ground," the leaps and manoeuvres practised in the air during the sixteenth to eighteenth centuries and that now, exceeding Olympic dressage standards by a long way, are the exclusive prerogative of the Spanish Riding School. To illustrate the difficulty involved, it takes four to six years for a rider to become proficient in these airs on a fully-trained horse and it will be two to four years more before he is capable of training a novice horse to this standard. Closely related to the Lipizzaner is the famous Kladruby Grey of Czechoslovakia, developed over the last three hundred years as the royal (now State) coach horse. Kladrubers have been known to draw a coach with up to sixteen horses in the traces, and have a pride and uniformity of movement which is the epitome of team-horse driving.

Driving as an art, as opposed to directing a carthorse or pony for an elementary function, is slightly less than 200 years old. It stems from the four-in-hands which used to pull stage coaches on the post roads, once the roads were made even enough to sustain a coach, and from the English fashion (much used by ladies at the turn of the eighteenth and nineteenth centuries) of taking the air in phaetons with a well-matched pair of elegant horses. Like dressage, it has nowadays become an art form, with the high-stepping hackney of the past predominant. It is a great attraction at horse shows throughout the world, and in its own right provides pleasure and a demanding skill for the driver.

All of these sports require an amateur to make them work; and "amateur" does not mean unprofessional, but loving.

Dressage is a field in which women excel as much as men.

Above left: Jennifer Loriston-Clarke, a superb British performer, bows to the judges during an indoor performance.

Above: The famous Spanish Riding School of Vienna (men only; both human and horse) performs a quadrille at home.

Left: A dressage contest for the not-quite-so-highly-advanced demonstrates some of the difficulties which can only be overcome by many years of practice. In this picture, the wishes of the riders can be seen from the way in which each sits his horse.

71

Some of the arts of driving are demonstrated in the varying types of pictures here.

Above left: Scurry racing requires a good deal of effort and precise judgement to manipulate a pair of cantering horses round a number of sharp turns.

Above: The hackney carriage driver concentrates her efforts on displaying her horse to best advantage.

Right: A Hungarian four-in-hand.

Left: Lippizaners, at the Piber Stud in Austria, are the perfect type of carriage horse, strong-bodied and elegant with a proud carriage. Although these are used exclusively by the Spanish Riding School, their first cousins, the Kladruby Greys of Czechoslovakia, provide the finest ceremonial coach team in the world.

Drums and Trumpets

Near the end of World War II the horse was used for the last time on the battlefield. Its active military career ended much as it had started, roughly 5,000 years before, with a Russian raid on an immobilized enemy. What had begun with hordes of Central Asian bowmen, on their rough steppe ponies, attacking horseless tribes finished with Russian cavalry divisions, also mounted on rough steppe ponies, demolishing the frozen-solid tanks of Germany with hand grenades, galloping away across the snow and leaving an enemy powerless to pursue.

In the five millennia between, horses had dominated warfare in many different ways. Much of the early fighting was done from chariots, giving the swordsman mobility and speed as well as a crudely protected fighting platform from which to swing down at his enemy's head. Drawn by two excited horses, in themselves enough to knock a foot soldier aside, many of these chariots carried built-in lethal weapons such as sharp knives embedded in the wheels which could cut an opponent's legs off.

It was not until the fourth century A.D. that the Romans replaced the primitive horsecloth with the padded saddle, adopted from the east, giving some security and physical comfort to archers and to mounted spearmen. But even before the development of the saddle, and indeed long after it—the North American Indian was fighting without a saddle until comparativily recently— hordes of skirmishing bowmen stayed on board successfully purely through balance and the strength of their leg muscles.

The invention of the stirrup, although known in Asia some 1,600 years ago, was not fully appreciated in Europe until the time of Charlemagne. Its adoption changed the course of warfare in two devastating ways. First, by providing a footboard against which the rider could brace his legs, the spear automatically became a lance —a thing to be aimed and held securely, with the full weight of the galloping horse behind it. Secondly, because the rider was to some extent artificially held in place by the harness of the horse he was able to wear cumbersome protective clothing which shielded him against he weapons of the enemy.

The Medieval Great Horse, famous forerunner of the carthorse of today, demonstrated more clearly than any horse has done before or since the ultimate benefit of the stirrup and the strong-built saddle. Knights in shining armor, jousting for fair ladies during peacetime and demolishing the heathen when the days of fun were over, not only wore so much protective armor that they had to be lifted on and off their horses but also carried behind their lances the thrust of the heaviest horse then known to man.

Meanwhile more clever and more psychological uses of horses

Left: British Household Cavalry drum horse Hercules of the Blues and Royals Regiment.

Right: The Blues and Royals (formerly known as the Horse Guards) line up for early morning Watering Order. The name derives from the old picket line practice of taking horses to water three times a day. Nowadays, since the horse is no longer used in battle, "Watering Order" has become synonymous with morning exercise. Interspersed with the ceremonial "Cavalry Blacks" are the Trumpeters' Greys of the regimental band.

were going forward. Genghis Khan's bloodthirsty raids into the Western world were based not on heavy armor but on a vast remuda of horses herded along with him, so that fresh mounts were always available to outdistance the enemy. (They also provided fresh meat and milk to keep his men in shape.) The victories of Cortés against the highly-civilized Aztecs came about very largely because the horse was then unknown in America. Man and horse were taken as one being (the centaur myth again) and an unknown race appearing out of the sea became the conquerors of the land. Only when the lance became redundant with the development of fire-power did the course of cavalry change again forever. Heavy armor was useless if a pistol ball could pierce it at close range; what mattered was physical freedom of movement, versatility, speed of horse to stop and start and turn away. From the early eighteenth century onwards light cavalry became the rule and the

Above left: A Household Cavalry Black loads up nervously in London. He is travelling to Edinburgh to form part of Queen Elizabeth's escort to greet the King of Sweden on a State Visit.

Above: The Life Guards march past to take part in the annual ceremony known as Trooping the Color, an historic spectacle in which, in the presence of Her Majesty the Queen, the regimental color is displayed so that a soldier lost on the battlefield knows which flag to come to.

Left: Ceremony carries on regardless of the weather. The Life Guards in the rain.

amazing arts of horsemanship exemplified by the Spanish Riding
School of Vienna came into their own.

All art forms pass, or fossilize into arts *per se*. The cavalry is
universally redundant, outweighed by new inventions that nullify
the horse's versatility and make his vulnerable mortality a hazard.
Yet, while hydrogen bombs may drop from 30,000 feet, the ceremonial
use of the warhorse, with its beauty and dignity, persists throughout
the world wherever grandeur and the continuity of tradition
are appreciated.

Both military and civil occasions will often feature mounted parades,
and horse soldiers play an important ceremonial role under very
different regimes: ancient monarchies, people's republics and
newly emergent states. They add color to daily life and often,
like those who draw the sightseers in London's streets, form an
important tourist attraction. Indeed, for some British state ceremonies
it is just as well that Elizabeth II is a capable horsewoman.

The British cavalry horse is very carefully selected and trained.
He will, most likely, be bought as a youngster from an Irish field;
chosen for his size and color by a buying commission made up
from officers of the British Army Veterinary Corps, the Household
Cavalry and the King's Troop Royal Horse Artillery who work
through selected agents and dealers who understand the Household
Cavalry's requirements.

Sent from Eire to Melton Mowbray in Leicestershire, the young
cavalry blacks are rested and grown for a week or a year until
a veterinary inspection clears them to move on to Windsor barracks,
where a toss of a coin decides whether they are destined for the
Horse Guards or the Life Guards. Once chosen, the number of the
new squadron they belong to is stamped on their hooves
(300 near-identical horses are difficult to tell apart, even to the most

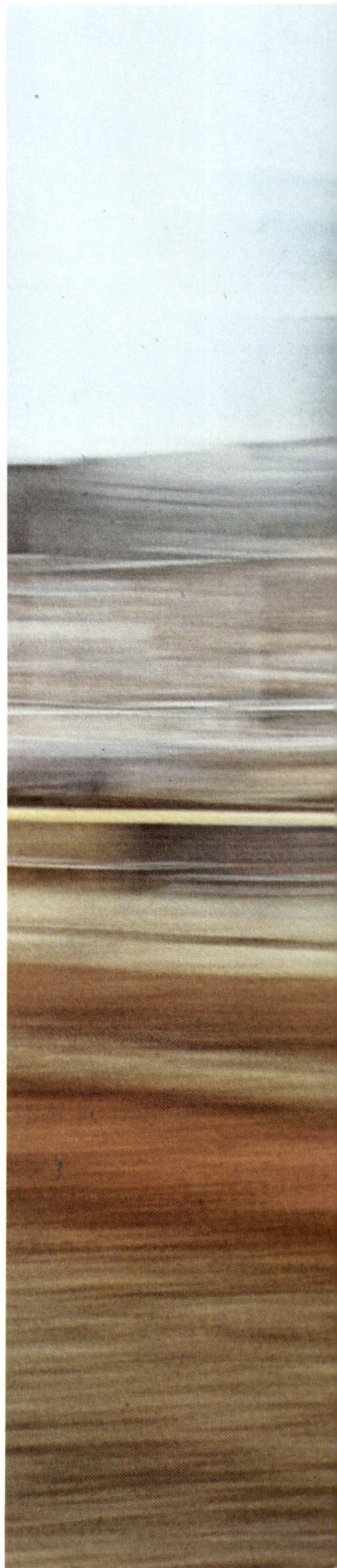

experienced horseman), and they are broken in and schooled on for three months or so until their basic training period is considered satisfactorily accomplished and they are shipped on to the barracks in London for more instruction in their future jobs. Nine out of ten of them develop into horses that will withstand the ebb and flow of ceremonial life, which says much for the men who bought them as youngsters, and the pick of these become officers' "chargers"— the most conspicuous on parade, and often as a sideline the best hunters or eventers or show jumpers that the cavalry can present. They lead a life that could make a film star quail, travelling from place to place, from country to country, to take part immaculately in British state occasions. When they retire—through old age or infirmity—they are often bought and cared for by a trooper who has come to love them. Otherwise, provided they are not in pain, they go out to grass to lead the easy, uneventful life of all respected old-age-pensioned warhorses.

Above: Royal Horse Artillery Wheelers pulling a light-weight gun carriage.

Below: Pageantry at a country show.

Right: Jousting, once a leading entertainment of the nobility, is coming back as a public spectacle.

The Hireling

Not so long ago, in one of the great American cities, I went riding. Friends, who were not themselves riders, had told me of a place where I could "go horseback riding" in much the same tones as they had earlier told me where I could rent a bicycle. This made me apprehensive that I was about to visit one of those establishments that can best be described as Rent-a-Horse.

Sure enough. "Ever been horseback riding before?" they asked me at the stable. I said I had and asked for a look round the yard, which they sent me off to do unaccompanied. I picked out the best two of the hundred or so horses, which seemed to surprise them. The owner said, "OK, you can take the gray," and without any more checking on my credentials saddled her up and sent me out on her without any supervision into some of the most dangerous streets in the world and from there into a park so small that you could ride twice round it in your $5-hour.

The gray was a nice little thing, sweet and fresh. I learned later that she had been bought by the stable less than a week before, which must have accounted for the fact that going round and round the same old park still interested her. From time to time untutored enthusiasts passed us on their hirelings. None of them was supervised by an instructor, and most were hanging on by the reins and banging up and down in the saddle. Two of them came by at a gallop on the street leading back to the stable.

I got back to the stable precisely on the hour, and as soon as I dismounted someone else got up on the gray mare and hauled her back to circle round the park. She did not know it then, but Rent-a-Horse had got her.

Six weeks later I went back to the same stable and asked for the gray mare. Her ears were back and her face was sour, and she tried to bite me when I patted her. She rode with an iron mouth and unresponsive sides, trying to duck out of going round the park and bolt back to the stable. Some months afterwards, when a kind of miserable curiosity impelled me to find out what had happened to her, I learned after a bit of digging that she had become unrideable and had been shot. She had been only six years old.

All over the world there are riding stables, dude ranches and pony trekking centers that are in the game only to make the maximum amount of money out of a horse in the shortest possible time.

RATES
1 HOUR 4.00 PONY RIDE .75
½ HOUR 3.00 OPEN DAILY

Ninety-nine per cent of their clients are people who genuinely want to learn how to ride, and who have no idea of the damage they do to the animals they ride. These novice riders are in no way to blame for the harm that is done through their agency. They, like the horses they hire, are the victims of profiteers who think of a horse as $5 an hour, 6 hours a day, 7 days a week, or $10,000 a year for as long as the horse can stick it.

Mercifully, the good riding establishments outnumber the bad. There is no better place to learn to ride than in a good riding school under a qualified instructor. A responsible riding school owner, having a number of horses in his charge, can choose one that will suit the size and ability of the pupil and can bring the novice rider on by degrees on a diversity of mounts, each of which will teach him something new.

Most countries have some sort of organized body, such as a horse society, which approves, or fails to approve, stables which offer horses for hire. Many of these will give out lists of approved schools on request. If the world's novice riders knew about these lists and took the advice given on them, Rent-a-Horse would go out of business. It cannot happen soon enough.

Horses at Work

Once upon a very recent time the economy of nations depended upon the strength and versatility of the horse. There were horses for carrying you about, horses upon which the morning post depended, horses for defending your country or for acquiring another one, horses for turning the ground for the young spring wheat, and horses for taking you to church on Sunday. If any of these horses broke down, the consequences were serious. If you weren't rich enough to own a horse you were stuck in your own backyard for the rest of your life. Most of the world was in that position, and the few who kept a horse for pleasure—that is, purely because they enjoyed riding about on it—must universally have been oddities.

In most parts of the world, despite a backdrop of almost universal automisation, the horse can still be found in use. There is the milk-float or the small trader's horse, pattering through some city streets in early morning, so much a part of everyday life that no one seems to notice him; the junk dealer, recognized by his cry, whose cart is pony-drawn and forms a regular and welcome change to the sound of changing gears; the hackney pair, pulling a smart carriage up a central thoroughfare, jangling above the rumble of the city traffic and usually used as much as an advertisement as for making deliveries. Those who look about them for a horse will always see one, standing perhaps as a genuine taxi service in Rome or at the south end of Central Park in Manhattan as a joy ride to escape the rush of modern city life.

Police horses patrol the streets of many cities, looking picturesque enough until the hysteria of a mob provokes their gentle firmness. I once stood in the path of 100 police horses sent in to control

Farm horses are still employed in France (*right*) and England (*below*).

30,000 demonstrators who were protesting against the Vietnam war. I simply wanted to see how the horse and the cop would handle me and had no political motive. The rider swung his truncheon at me, failing it score because it wasn't long enough to reach beyond his horse's head. What the well-trained horse did was very curious: it moved its front feet, gently but firmly, *under* my shoes and not on top, stuck its nose against my chest, and quietly but irresistably forced me backwards. This horse had just moved out from a line which were having firecrackers thrown at them.

In many high-altitude areas, where cold or a tortuous pathway render any sort of motor vehicle unusable, the horse performs its age-old function of packing home the groceries, delivering the homestead produce into the valley market; and adds to this a thriving tourist business such as getting down the side of the Grand Canyon in Arizona, which is far beyond the capability of the jeep or Range-Rover.

Ecologically, the plough horse has seemed to be redundant. But with the rising cost of motor fuel and the limits of fuel supplies that are pushing prices up beyond the profit of running the machine he is beginning to come back into his own. What for a brief period

Left: Roping a steer in the United States.

Below: Australian cowboy

Right: Royal Canadian Mounted Police present a display.

of time has been forgotten is that the horse lives off the land he works, eating its produce, enriching it with his manure, and meanwhile expending his energy without charge into an agricultural economy that is severely set back by the much-faster depreciation rate of each new tractor bought and worked. Repair bills for a horse are minimal compared with complications to a combine harvester, and the owner is not nearly so dependent on the interplay of public services. Any speculator of the future is bound about with supposition. No matter: my own bet, failing the widespread use of self-generating electric batteries or some such cheap invention, is that with the exhaustion of world fuel supplies the self-generating horse will come back into his own.

Alternatively, it may be the mule (offspring of a male donkey

Left top: Picadors in the bull ring at Palma de Mallorca. The horses are protected (at least, to some extent) by padded blankets reaching almost to the ground.

Left: An Arab working in a circus. Dressage displays are popular with the crowd.

Right: The polo pony is a thriving reminder of an ancient game: polo was played in China and Mongolia many centuries ago. Today most of the world's polo ponies are bred in Argentina, which has about three times as many polo players as any other country. Since they need to be 15 hands high, or a little taller, they are not strictly speaking ponies at all.

and a mare) which holds the premium. This is an animal which has never reached redundancy, being excessively cheap to maintain, extraordinarily enduring, and possessed of so deep an ability to hang around indefinitely that the word "mulish" has become part of the universal tongue. It is seen throughout the Mediterranean countries, dragging a plough through the dried-out soil of Moorish terraces or standing patiently beneath the almond trees waiting for the ripening crop to fall into its panniers, but it cannot be produced without the horse.

Working horses endure in the present as they have throughout the past. Where would Indonesia be without the strength of its Sumba or Sumbawa ponies, or most of mid- and eastern-Asia without its Mongolian strains? All modern horses work, in the sense that riding for pleasure is a concept of the passenger and not of the means of locomotion. Even the most expensive racehorse works long before he reaches puberty, and at stud in later years is never pensioned off until his/her working value it proven to have disappeared.

Horses exist, and will continue to exist, only as long as they have value to man. It is in the way of things—in the way of a dominant species on a small planet that is part of a limited universe—that existence should depend on such precarious factors.

The horse's working use is still diverse.

Above left: Pack horse in Yugoslavia.

Above centre: Threshing wheat in Greece.

Above: Drawing a festive fiacre in Vienna.

Far right: Ploughing in Germany.

Right: The Roman carrozza is now largely a tourist attraction.

Below, left and center: It is often the only means of transport in Nepal and Afghanistan (respectively).

Below: The winter taxi in Zermatt is often a necessity in heavy weather.

Top left: Anything goes in the shafts in China, provided it will work.

Top centre: Mountain sleigh in Bavaria.

Top right: Horses in Yugoslavia.

Above: A fisherman's cart collecting cockles on the beach in Lancashire, England.

Right center: Mules are a common sight in all Mediterranean countries. These are in Andalusia, Spain.

Right: A farm horse in Turkey.

Below centre: These mules are Greek.

Below right: German dray horses.

92

End of the Day

Therefore my age is as the lusty winter
Frosty, but kindly.

William Shakespeare:
As You Like It

The oldest horse on record, Old Billy, a barge horse who used
to pull the barges on the waterways of England when shipment
by canal was very much the thing and the railways had not taken over,
died at the age of 62. Four years of a horse's life are said to equal
one year for·a human, so Old Billy survived to the equivalent of 248,
which would make a tortoise feel like a babe-in-arms.
Horses, averagely, live to about 25 years. There are some curious
similes about a horse's age which have become part of the language
of man: if they get "much longer in the tooth" (horses' teeth
continue growing, humans' don't) they go to "fresh fields and
pastures new." One of the most common ways of achieving this
is by being put down, sometimes because they have outlived their
usefulness but more often because they develop geriatric complaints
such as arthritis or not being able to masticate properly because their
teeth are too long and angled out to chew their food. Putting an end
to it may be a whole lot better than protracting their discomfort.

Certainly, in natural circumstances, they would lose contact
with the herd through sheer inability to keep up, probably dying
by human standards rather nastily over a period of several days.
The difficulty of applying human standards is that they are
only human. There comes a point in every healthy horse's life
when a human decides that he is too old to work. At this point
he is either put down or retired; and since a good many years
may remain to him to enjoy, it is pleasing when he is given
the opportunity to revert to a natural (but protected) way of life.
Throughout the world, though limited by finance, homes for
old horses exist in which the herd instinct that wants company
is automatically satisfied and in addition there is shelter against
rough weather, extra food when the grass dies down, and
medical attention.
Under such circumstances the ripening years provoke a kind
of reverence. Old Billy must have drawn the admiration of all who saw
him for the last quarter-century of his life, but it is hardly likely
that he guessed at what it was they wondered.

The ultimate luxury for the old horse. A retirement home gives rest
and care to horses and ponies of all types.

Acknowledgements

The publisher would like to thank the following for supplying the photographs reproduced in this book:
Anne Cumbers page 11*t*, 15*b*, 20*t*, 20*bl*, 21*t*, 24*bl*, 25*c*, 25*bl*, 68*t*, 84; Robert Estall page 12-13, 14, 16*t*, 21*b*, 25*t*, 26*l*, 28-29, 30*b*, 36, 37, 38-39, 45*c*, 50*b*, 52*t*, 52-53, 63, 65, 71*t*, 73*t*, 74, 82, 85, 87, 96; Paul Forrester page 38, 39, 59*b*, 61, 75, 76*t*; Robert Harding Associates page 76*b*, 78*t*, 90*bl*, 90*br*, 92*t*, 93*bl*, 95*b*; Alan Hutchison page 31*b*, 56, 78*b*, 79*r*, 92*b*; Ed Lacey page 44*t*, 45*t*; John Moss page 19, 26*c*, 26*r*, 60, 83*t*; Picturepoint page 7*l*, 7*r*, 8; Spectrum Colour Library page 1, 2-3, 4-5, 10, 11*b*, 20*br*, 27, 30*t*, 33, 34*t*, 34*b*, 35*b*, 40*t*, 42-43, 45*b*, 80*t*, 80*b*, 81, 91*b*, 92*c*, 93*c*, 94, 95*t*; Sally-Anne Thompson page 16*b*, 25*br*, 31*t*, 58*l*, 58*r*, 64*t*, 66*t*, 66*b*, 67*t*, 67*b*, 72*t*; ZEFA page 6, 9*b*, 15*t*, 17, 18, 22*t*, 22-23, 24*t*, 24*br*, 32, 35*t*, 40*c*, 40-41, 44*b*, 46-47, 48*b*, 49, 50*t*, 51, 54-55, 57, 59*t*, 64*b*, 68*b*, 69*b*, 70, 71*b*, 73*b*, 77, 78-79*t*, 78-79*b*, 83*b*, 86*b*, 88*t*, 90*tl*, 90*tr*, 90*c*, 91*t*, 91*c*, 93*tl*, 93*tr*, 93*br*; ZEFA/Photri page 68*t*.

The publishers have attempted to observe the legal requirements with respect to the rights of the suppliers of photographic materials. Nevertheless, persons who have claims are invited to apply to the Publishers.